CIVILIZATIONS

OF AFRICA

THE
MASAI
OF EAST AFRICA

Jamie Hetfield

W
FRANKLIN WATTS
NEW YORK • LONDON • SYDNEY

This edition first published in the UK in 1997 by
Franklin Watts
96 Leonard Street
London
EC2A 4RH

© 1996 The Rosen Publishing Group, Inc., New York

Picture credits: Cover © CFM, Nairobi; p. 4 © Buddy Mays/International Stick;
pp. 7, 15 © G. E. Pakenham/International Stock; pp. 8, 16 © Wendy Stone/Gamma Liaison;
pp. 11, 12 © David Cimino/International Stock;
p. 19 © Seena Sussman/International Stock; p. 20 © Chad Ehlers/International Stock.

A CIP catalogue record for this book is available from the British Library.

ISBN 0 7496 2859 6

Printed in the United States of America

Contents

The Masai of East Africa

The **Masai** live on the **savannahs** of East Africa. These are grasslands that stretch as far as you can see.

In the eastern part of these savannahs is **Mount Kilimanjaro**. It is the highest mountain in Africa. Snow covers the top for most of the year.

Wild animals such as lions, zebras, elephants and antelope also live on the savannahs.

◀ The savannahs are the traditional homelands of the Masai.

How the Masai live

The Masai are a proud people.
Their warriors are famous for their strength
and courage.

The Masai keep large herds of cattle.
The herds roam the savannahs in search
of grass and water. The Masai go with
them to take care of them.

The Masai get milk, meat and leather
from their cattle.

The Masai follow their cattle ▶
across the savannahs.

Homes

When a group of Masai move to a new place, they build a small village.
The men make a high circular fence of thornbushes. The prickly branches protect them from **predators** and cattle thieves.

Inside the fence the women build houses out of grass and mud. In the centre of the village is an open space where the cattle are kept at night.

◀ Masai women build homes for their families to live in.

9

Food

The Masai's main food is milk from their cows. Warriors drink blood from the cattle to make them strong. A woman who has just had a baby also drinks the blood to bring her strength back. The Masai only eat the meat of their cattle on very special occasions.

The Masai buy other food, such as sugar and bread, from shops in nearby towns.

Drinking cows' blood helps a new ▶
mother regain her strength.

Clothes

The Masai wear long cotton clothes, usually coloured red, orange or brown. Some have bright stripes and patterns.

They also wear necklaces and earrings made of blue, orange and red beads.

On special occasions the Masai paint their bodies with a mixture of earth and a kind of clay called **ochre**.

◀ Both Masai men and women wear beautiful jewellery.

13

Children

All children learn how to take care of their family's herds by looking after the young animals.

Children are taught to sing to the cattle and to recognize that each cow has its own personality.

Children can soon tell the cattle apart by the different shapes of their horns and the different colours of their skins.

Looking after the family's cattle is ▶ an important task.

A wedding day

A wedding is an important occasion.
The bride and her family shave their heads.
They wear clothes of soft leather and
their finest necklaces.

Then the groom leads the bride and
her family to his house. When she gets to
her new home, the bride is given gifts
of milk, meat and honey.

The day ends with everyone singing
and dancing.

◀ The bride's mother drips milk on the bride's feet as
part of the wedding ceremony.

17

Becoming a warrior

A Masai boy becomes a warrior when
he is about 14 years old. A few years later,
as a test of manhood, he goes into
the wild alone. There he hopes to kill
a lion. If he does, he wears the lion's **mane**
as a headdress.

Warriors are fearless protectors of their
people. They are brave and strong,
but they are also gentle.

Masai warriors are famous for their dances ▶
where they jump very high in the air.

Kenya and Tanzania

The savannahs where the Masai live form part of the countries of **Kenya** and **Tanzania**.

About 26 million people live in Kenya and about 28 million people live in Tanzania.

The capital of Kenya is Nairobi and the capital of Tanzania is Dodoma.

◀ Some Masai have moved to cities such as Nairobi.

Changing times

Today, it is difficult for the Masai to follow their **traditional** ways. The laws in their countries make it hard for them to roam with their herds.

Many Masai now live and work in towns and no longer have cattle. Their children go to school, like you.

But wherever the Masai live, they are still proud to be Masai.

Glossary

Kenya   Country in East Africa.

Masai   A people who live in East Africa.

mane   Thick hair around a male lion's face.

Mount Kilimanjaro Highest mountain in Africa.

ochre   Type of clay that can be made into coloured body paint.

predator   Wild animal that lives by eating other animals.

savannah Large area of grassland.

traditional The way people have done things for a long time.

Tanzania Country in East Africa.

23

Index